Why Animals Don't Get Heart Attacks

...But Humans Do

Matthias Rath, M.D.

Published and Distributed by Health Now
387 Ivy Street, San Francisco, CA 94102 U.S.A.
Tel. 1-800-624-2442

ISBN 0-9638768-1-3

Why This Book Will Change Your Life

- **Every second person dies from heart attacks or strokes.** According to the World Health Organization, more than 12 million people die every year worldwide from heart attacks, strokes, and other forms of cardiovascular diseases. These deaths are largely preventable.

- **But animals don't get heart attacks and strokes.** This book gives you the answer to why animals don't get heart attacks and it will tell why the answer to this puzzle will lead to the eradication of cardiovascular disease among human beings.

- **Heart attacks and strokes are not diseases — they are caused by vitamin deficiencies.** America's number one killer can be prevented by an optimum intake of essential nutrients. This book tells you the essential nutrients to optimize your cardiovascular health.

- **The world's first patented therapy to reverse heart disease without surgery.** The recommendations made in this book can not only help you to prevent cardiovascular disease; they can also help those readers with existing coronary heart disease and other forms of cardiovascular disease to reverse it.

- **A daily program of cellular essentials contributing to optimum cardiovascular health for everyone.** In most people, blood vessel deposits start developing already during their twenties. The cardiovascular health program presented here can improve the health of millions of people in a natural way — from their twenties to their nineties.

- **Striking testimonials from people already following this program.** Any preventive program is best tested under severe conditions. You will read grateful letters from patients with existing heart conditions following this program. Patients with angina pectoris, irregular heartbeat, heart failure, high blood pressure, diabetes and other diseases report dramatic improvements or complete disappearance of their problems.

- **A medical breakthrough will make an old dream of mankind come true.** Heart attacks and other forms of cardiovascular disease can essentially become unknown during this generation and forthcoming generations.

- **This book is an authentic report. Most health books summarize the work of other people — this book is different.** The author of this book is privileged to have led the scientific and medical breakthrough toward the eradication of heart disease. He discovered that all genetic disorders leading to heart disease are closely associated with vitamin deficiencies. Moreover, he discovered that all risk factors known today in clinical cardiology which increase the risk for cardiovascular disease are associated with vitamin deficiencies. His best-selling book, *Eradicating Heart Disease,* is the authentic report about these discoveries. This book, *Why Animals Don't Get Heart Disease,* is a practical health guide for everyone.

This Book Is Your Opportunity

This book is an invitation to take advantage of a lifetime opportunity.

- **Optimize your own health.** By following the cardiovascular health program of this book you can take advantage of the most advanced natural nutritional program to live longer and to stay healthy.

- **Help to improve the health of others.** By reading this book you will realize it's important not only for yourself but for your family, your friends, neighbors and many other people you know.

- **Experience for yourself and use your own judgment.** The information in this book has two invincible advantages: First, it is scientifically based, and second, it is strikingly logical. Everyone can understand the message of this book. Experience the difference for yourself.

- **Take the challenge.** Just as any other breakthrough in science and medicine the information in this book is new. Because of that it has to gradually replace existing medical dogmas. Be prepared. You will face questions, skepticism; perhaps, even opposition. The more someone is personally or economically dependent on existing dogmas, the more resistance they will put up against this breakthrough. Take the challenge. The logical information of this book has the power of a nuclear bomb. Within a few years it will change the way *everyone* sees heart disease.

- **Take this book and help to spread this life-saving information.** The first clinical studies that vitamin deficiencies are primary risk factors for heart disease were already published in 1941 — more than half a century ago. The life-saving information from these studies was swept under the carpet of negligence and oblivion, primarily because vitamins are not patentable. Because of that fact more than half a billion people died — prematurely. It is time for a change. Now that the scientific rationale has been discovered, eradicating heart disease has become a realistic goal. How fast we achieve this goal is primarily dependent on one factor: how fast can we spread this information?

- **Become part of a historic development.** I invite you to become part of a historic process toward the eradication of heart disease. Talk about this book to your friends and in your community. Talk about the scientific discoveries reported in it. Talk about its logic. Contribute to one of the great steps forward for human health. You can make all the difference. Imagine the pride in your eyes when you tell your children and grandchildren: we did it, and I was part of it!

Dr. Rath's Ten-Step Program
to Optimum Cardiovascular Health

1. **Be aware of the size and function of your cardiovascular system.** Did you know that your blood vessel pipeline system measures 60,000 miles and is the largest organ in your body? Did do know that your heart pumps 100,000 times every day performing the greatest amount of work of all organs? Optimizing your cardiovascular health benefits your entire body and your overall health. Optimizing your cardiovascular health adds years to your life because your body is as old as your cardiovascular system.

2. **Stabilize the walls of your blood vessels.** Blood vessel instability and lesions in your blood vessel walls are primary causes for cardiovascular disease. Vitamin C is the cement of the blood vessel walls and stabilizes them. Animals don't get heart disease because they produce enough endogenous vitamin C in their livers to protect their blood vessels. In contrast, we humans develop deposits leading to heart attacks and strokes because we cannot manufacture endogenous vitamin C and generally get too few vitamins in our diet.

3. **Reverse existing deposits in your arteries without surgery**. Cholesterol and fat particles are deposited inside the blood vessel walls by means of biological adhesives. Teflon-like agents can prevent this stickiness. The amino acids lysine and proline are nature's teflon agents. Together with vitamin C they help reverse existing deposits naturally.

4. **Relax your blood vessel walls.** Deposits and spasms of the blood vessel walls are the cause of high blood pressure. Dietary supplementation of magnesium (nature's calcium antagonist) and vitamin C relax the blood vessel walls and normalize high blood pressure. The natural amino acid arginine can be of additional value.

5. **Optimize the performance of your heart**. The heart is the motor of the cardiovascular system. Like the motor of a car, the millions of muscle cells need cell fuel for optimum performance. Nature's cell fuels include: Carnitine, coenzyme Q-10, B vitamins, many nutrients and trace elements. Dietary supplementation of these essential nutrients will optimize the pumping performance of the heart and contribute to a regular heartbeat.

6. **Protect your cardiovascular pipeline from rusting**. Biological rusting, or oxidation, damages your cardiovascular system and accelerates the aging process. Vitamin C, vitamin E, beta carotene and selenium are the most important natural antioxidants. Other important antioxidants are bioflavonoids such as pycnogenol. Dietary supplementation of these antioxidants provides important rust protection for your cardiovascular system. Above all, stop smoking, because cigarette smoke accelerates the rusting of your blood vessels.

7. **Exercise regularly.** Regular physical activity is an important element of any

cardiovascular health program. Moderate and regular exercise, like walking or bicycling, is ideal and can be performed by everybody.

8. **Eat a prudent diet.** The diet of our ancestors over thousands of generations shaped our metabolism and from it we can learn what is best for our bodies today. Their diet was rich in plant nutrition and high in fiber and vitamins. A diet rich in fruits and vegetables enhances your cardiovascular health today.

9. **Find time to relax.** Physical and emotional stress are cardiovascular risk factors. Schedule hours and days to relax as you would schedule your appointments. You should also know that the production of the stress hormone adrenaline uses up your body's vitamin C supply. Long-term physical or emotional stress depletes your vitamin body pool and requires dietary vitamin supplementation.

10. **Start now.** Thickening of the blood vessel walls is not only a problem of the elderly — it starts early in life. Studies have shown that first blood vessel deposits develop before age 20. Start protecting your cardiovascular system now. The earlier you start, the more years you will add to your life.

This 10-step program to optimum cardiovascular health will be described in greater detail throughout this book, but first let's have a closer look at the underlying problem of cardiovascular disease.

Effective, Safe and Affordable Cardiovascular Health

This book presents the ultimate cardiovascular health program. It combines lifestyle changes with a daily nutritional supplement program. Why is this combination so important?

A prudent diet and regular exercise are the basis for a healthy cardiovascular lifestyle. Yet, we have to understand that lifestyle changes *alone* do not address many of the key problems necessary to maintain and to restore cardiovascular health in our body. Some of the problems not addressed by lifestyle changes are the stability of the blood vessel walls, natural teflon-like protection for blood vessel walls, antioxidant protection, cell fuel for millions of heart and blood vessel cells. Moreover, in many cases like in heart failure patients on a waiting list for a heart transplant operation, exercise and other lifestyle changes are no option at all.

This is why a combination of lifestyle changes with an optimum nutritional supplement program will turn out to be the ultimate cardiovascular health program for the future. The cardiovascular health program presented in this book is scientifically formulated to contribute to optimum cardiovascular health for everyone.

Finally, the more people follow this program, the more money can be saved in health care costs. By spreading the message of this book you can contribute to a health care reform that has the right focus — prevention.

Cardiovascular Disease Kills Every Second Person

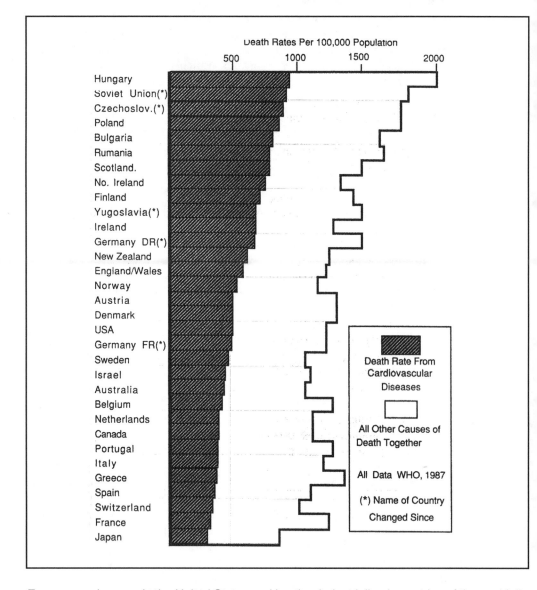

Death Rates Per 100,000 Population

Every second person in the United States and in other industrialized countries of the world die from heart attacks, strokes and other forms of cardiovascular disease, men and women alike. According to the latest statistics of the World Health Organization, more than 12 million die every year from this disease. Cardiovascular disease has become the plague of the 20th century. The adjacent figure shows that the cardiovascular epidemic rages all over the globe. France, Greece and a few other southern European countries are the exception. The main factor contributing to the low heart disease rate in these countries is the natural, vitamin-rich diet.

The Nature of Cardiovascular Disease

Cardiovascular disease comprises all diseases affecting the heart (cardio-) and the blood vessel (vascular) system, including coronary heart disease, heart failure, arrhythmia and others. Atherosclerosis, the buildup of deposits in the blood vessel wall, is by far the most frequent among all these problems. Since the atherosclerotic deposits develop primarily in the arteries of the heart (coronary arteries) the terms coronary heart disease and cardiovascular disease are frequently substituting each other. To simplify things, we will talk about cardiovascular diseases throughout this book.

The adjacent picture shows the core of the problem. What you see are cross-sections through coronary arteries. Imagine you are looking through a microscope into the blood vessels: this is what you would see. The dark ring you notice is the original blood vessel wall as it would be found in a newborn baby. Everything else develops after birth. The gray area within this dark ring are atherosclerotic deposits, which narrow the blood flow through this artery.

Figure A: Imagine a patient coming into the doctor's office and complaining about angina pectoris, the chest pain typical for coronary heart disease. This is how his coronary arteries would look. Over many years fat particles and other risk factors from the blood have entered the walls of this patient's arteries and led to the buildup of atherosclerotic deposits. These deposits considerably narrow the blood flow through these coronary arteries, thereby reducing the oxygen and nutrient supply to millions of heart muscle cells nourished from this artery. The suffocation of these millions of cells, particularly when the patient undergoes physical exercise, causes the sharp chest pain. Thus, angina pectoris is nothing else than the suffocation "cry" of millions of heart muscle cells projected to the outside of the body.

Figure B. Imagine a patient who had just had a heart attack. He is transported in an ambulance to the intensive care unit of a clinic. This is how his coronary arteries would look. What has happened? On top of the atherosclerotic deposits, a blood clot has now formed completely interrupting the blood flow through his arteries. As a result, the portion of the heart which is nourished by this artery dies off and ceases to function. A heart attack can be compared to the failure of a motor. The failure of one cylinder in a four-cylinder motor impairs the overall performance of the motor and the car. The same effect has a heart attack on the performance of the heart and the body of the patient. In one out of three patients the impairment of the heart muscle cells after a heart attack is so severe that the patient dies before getting medical attention.

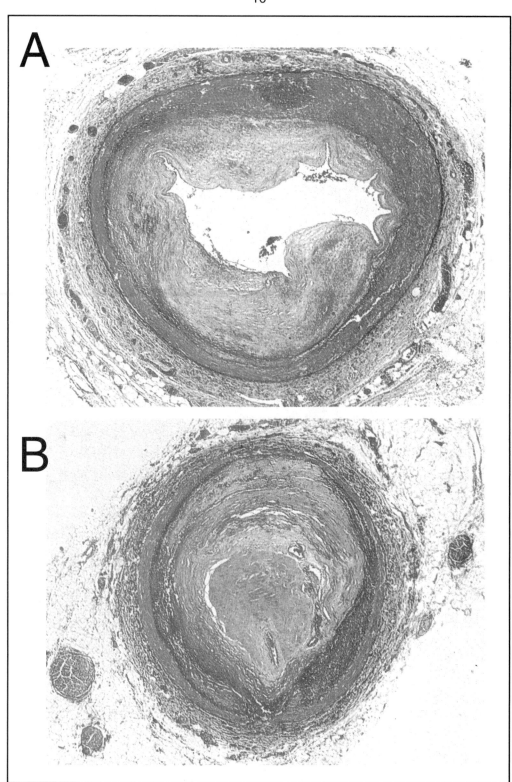

Blood Vessel Deposits Develop Early in Life

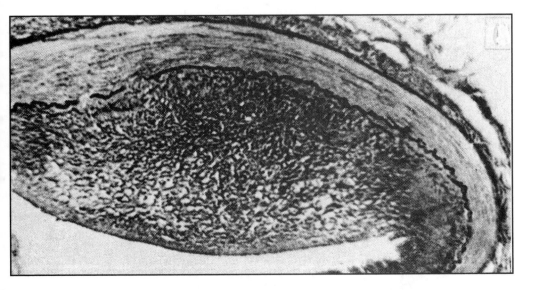

Atherosclerotic deposits and cardiovascular disease are not limited to advanced age. Studies of soldiers killed in the Korean and Vietnam wars showed that up to 75% of the victims studied had already developed some form of atherosclerotic deposits — at age 25 and younger. These dramatic findings were confirmed in young victims of traffic accidents. These figures are alarming and the message is clear: it is never early enough to start protecting your cardiovascular system.

The picture above needs no further interpretation. It shows the coronary artery of a 25-year-old victim of a car accident. The atherosclerotic deposits you see may have reduced the blood flow through this person's arteries by 50% — even at that early age. Such large deposits at age 25 are the exception. Unfortunately, we generally don't know the size — until it is too late.

Among all puzzles of medicine this is the most striking one: While over 12 million people die from heart attacks and strokes every year, cardiovascular disease is essentially unknown in billions of other living beings on this planet. Animals don't get heart attacks.

The Striking Fact: Animals Don' t Get Heart Attacks

The fact remains, however, that in none of the domestic species, with the rarest of exceptions, do animals develop arteriosclerotic diseases of clinical significance.

It appears that most of the pertinent pathological mechanisms operate in animals and that arteriosclerotic disease in them is not impossible; <u>it just does not occur.</u>

If the reason for this could be found, it might cast some very useful light on the human disease.

Prof. H.A. Smith, Prof. T.C. Jones
***Textbook of Veterinary Pathology,* 1958**

The fact that animals rarely get heart attacks and strokes is little known. This is even more surprising since this fact is well established in the scientific literature. Above you will find a quote from the *Textbook of Veterinary Pathology* written by two professors, H.A. Smith and T.C. Jones in 1958. This textbook summarizes observations about diseases in animals. The chapter on cardiovascular disease is relatively short. The basic message is: animals don't get heart disease. "It just does not occur. If the reason for this could be found it might cast some very useful light on the human disease." Of course, some animals may develop cardiovascular complications at old age, shortly before they die. However, cardiovascular disease as it affects millions of people in the midst of their lives, hardly ever occurs in animals.

This above observation was published in 1958. Now, over three decades later, the main reason why animals don't get heart attacks has been found. Animals manufacture their own daily vitamin C supply in their livers, while we human beings have lost this ability.

Why Animals Don't Get Heart Attacks

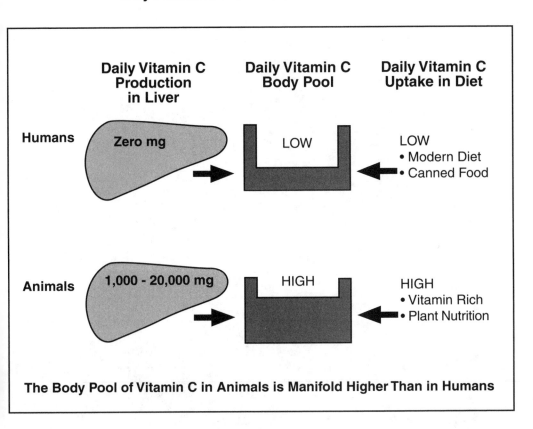

Animals don't get heart attacks because they are able to manufacture high amounts of vitamin C in their bodies. Every day animals convert between 1,000 and 20,000 milligrams of sugar molecules into vitamin C molecules, when compared to the human body weight. In addition, animals also increase their body pool of vitamin C by vitamin-rich plant nutrition.

In contrast, we human beings cannot manufacture our own vitamin C. Our ancestors lost this ability thousands of generations ago. Thus, all human beings living today are dependent on getting enough vitamin C in our diet. Unfortunately, our modern diet contains insufficient amounts of vitamins. Even worse, food processing and cooking destroy much of the vitamins originally present in the food. The single most important difference between the metabolism of human beings and 99% of all other living species is the dramatic difference in the body pool of vitamin C.

How does vitamin C prevent cardiovascular diseases?

Vitamin C Reinforces the Walls of Our Blood Vessels

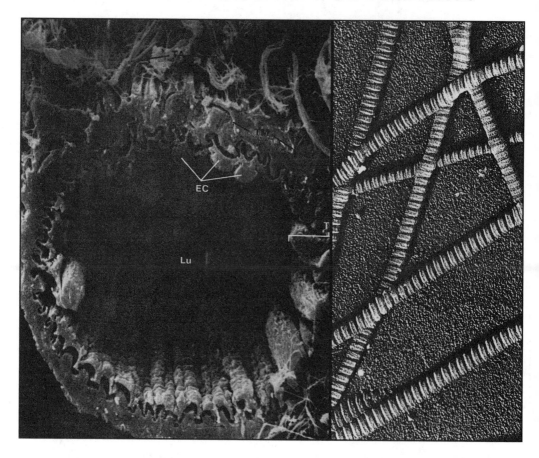

Why is vitamin C so important? How does it prevent cardiovascular disease? Vitamin C contributes in many different ways to the prevention of cardiovascular disease. It is an important antioxidant in our body, and it serves as a co-factor for many biochemical reactions. The most important function of vitamin C, however, is to stimulate the production of collagen, elastin and other reinforcement molecules in our body. These biological reinforcement rods constitute the connective tissue in our body — about 50% of all proteins in our body. The more collagen produced, the more stability for our bones, the skin — and for the 60,000-mile-long walls of our arteries, veins and capillaries.

Above on the left, you see a cross-section of a human artery under the microscope. Everything white represents collagen and other connective tissue. We can see that our blood vessels get their principal shape and stability from these reinforcement molecules. On the right hand side, under higher magnification, you see individual collagen fibrils. Each of these biological reinforcement molecules is stronger than an iron wire of comparable width. The connection between vitamin C deficiency and instability of the blood vessels is long established (see following page). Unfortunately, the next logical step has not been recognized until now: cardiovascular disease is nothing else than an early form of scurvy.

The Scientific World Knows the Facts

The importance of vitamin C for the stability of the human body has been recognized long ago. Below you will see the reprint of a page from Dr. Lubert Stryers *Biochemistry,* one of the leading textbooks which helps to educate generations of scientists in universities around the world. While the vitamin C collagen connection is firmly established, the paramount importance of this vitamin for heart disease has apparently been overlooked or neglected.

DEFECTIVE HYDROXYLATION IS ONE OF THE BIOCHEMICAL LESIONS IN SCURVY

The importance of the hydroxylation of collagen becomes evident in *scurvy*. A vivid description of this disease was given by Jacques Cartier in 1536, when it afflicted his men as they were exploring the Saint Lawrence River:

> Some did lose all their strength, and could not stand on their feet. . . . Others also had all their skins spotted with spots of blood of a purple colour: then did it ascend up to their ankles, knees, thighs, shoulders, arms, and necks. Their mouths became stinking, their gums so rotten, that all the flesh did fall off, even to the roots of the teeth, which did also almost all fall out.

The means of preventing scurvy was succinctly stated by James Lind, a Scottish physician, in 1753:

> Experience indeed sufficiently shows that as greens or fresh vegetables, with ripe fruits, are the best remedies for it, so they prove the most effectual preservatives against it.

Lind urged the inclusion of lemon juice in the diet of sailors. His advice was adopted by the British Navy some forty years later.

Scurvy is caused by a dietary deficiency of ascorbic acid (vitamin C). Primates and guinea pigs have lost the ability to synthesize ascorbic acid and so they must acquire it from their diets. Ascorbic acid, an effective reducing agent (Figure 11-13), maintains prolyl hydroxylase in an active form, probably by keeping its iron atom in the reduced ferrous state. Collagen synthesized in the absence of ascorbic acid is insufficiently hydroxylated and hence has a lower melting temperature. This abnormal collagen cannot properly form fibers and thus causes the skin lesions and blood-vessel fragility that are so prominent in scurvy.

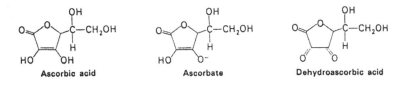

Ascorbic acid   Ascorbate   Dehydroascorbic acid

Cardiovascular Disease is an Early Form of Scurvy

The following figure summarizes an important discovery: cardiovascular disease is an early form of scurvy. The atherosclerotic deposits are nothing else than nature's "plaster cast" to stabilize a weakened blood vessel wall. If this repair process overshoots, or overcompensates, cardiovascular disease develops. The adjacent figure is so logical that it may soon become part of the educational material for many schools around the world.

Column A. We already know that vitamin C increases the production of collagen molecules. A reinforced blood vessel wall does not allow deposits to develop. The cross-section through a vitamin C-reinforced blood vessel reveals a blood vessel pipeline without deposits. This is why animals don't get heart attacks.

Column C. On the right hand side of this figure, you see something else that is familiar: scurvy. Scurvy is a deadly disease caused by the total depletion of vitamin C in the body. Gum bleeding is the first sign of unstable and leaky blood vessels. Thousands of sailors died during the ship voyages of earlier centuries from hemorrhagic blood loss through leaky blood vessel walls throughout their bodies. Zero vitamin C intake leads to death within four to six months.

Column B. Cardiovascular disease lies exactly between these two conditions. Our average diet contains enough vitamin C to prevent open scurvy, but not enough vitamin C to guarantee a stable, reinforced blood vessel wall. As a consequence, over many years, cracks, lesions and gaps occur in the inside of the artery walls. With low vitamin C intake these lesions don't heal. Instead, cholesterol, fat globules and other blood factors enter the blood vessel wall in order to *repair* these lesions. With chronically low vitamin C intake, this repair process continues over many years; it overshoots and atherosclerotic deposits develop. Local growth of cells inside the vessel wall further increases these deposits. Deposits in the arteries of the heart lead to heart attacks, deposits in the arteries of the brain lead to stroke.

Optimum daily intake of vitamin C in our diet stabilizes the walls of the blood vessels and helps prevent heart attacks and strokes.

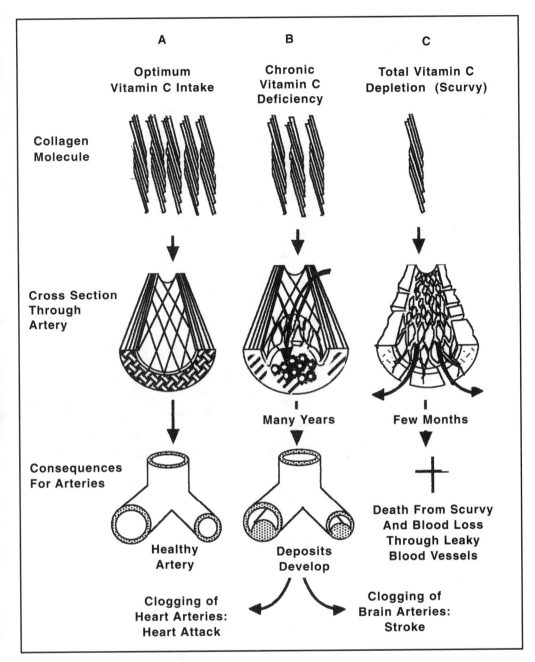

Why the Ship Cats Did Not Get Scurvy

During long ship voyages of early centuries up to 90% of the sailors died from scurvy. Astonishingly, while the majority of sailors had to be buried at sea, ship cats and other animals aboard stayed alive and returned healthy. This phenomenon puzzled the admiralties of the seafaring nations over centuries. Today, the explanation to this puzzle is simple.

The ship cats and other animals aboard did not die from scurvy because these animals produced their own vitamin C. The reason why the animals aboard did not get scurvy *then* is the same reason why animals don't get heart attacks *today* — their blood vessels are reinforced by endogenous vitamin C production. The reason why tens of thousands of sailors died from scurvy *then* is the same reason why humans are prone to cardiovascular disease *today*. Chronic vitamin C deficiency causes weakness of our blood vessel walls.

Vitamin C Deficiency Directly Causes
Atherosclerotic Deposits and Cardiovascular Disease

We now have to prove that the lack of one single factor in the diet, vitamin C, directly causes heart attack, strokes and other forms of cardiovascular disease. How could we prove this? For obvious reasons, this test cannot be performed in human beings. It would simply be unethical to deplete a volunteer of vitamins and wait until a heart attack or a stroke occurs.

Luckily, there is another way. Although 99% of animals produce their own vitamin C, there are a few exceptions, one of which is the guinea pig. Thus, the most direct way to get an answer to this question was to design a study in this animal model to answer the following question: What happens to the artery walls of guinea pigs if they get little vitamin C in their diet over a period of time? We therefore designed the following experiment:

We divided a set of guinea pigs into two groups. One group received 60 milligrams of vitamin C in their diet, compared to human body weight. This amount was chosen to mimic the official recommended daily allowance for humans. The second set of guinea pigs received about 5,000 milligrams of vitamin C per day. All other factors in the diet, cholesterol, fat, sugar, sodium, etc., were the same. After five weeks the arteries of both groups of animals were analyzed. The results were rather dramatic. The picture on the next page is part of the patents approved by the U.S. Patent Office for the prevention and treatment of cardiovascular disease.

The Proof - Vitamin C Deficiency Can Cause Heart Disease

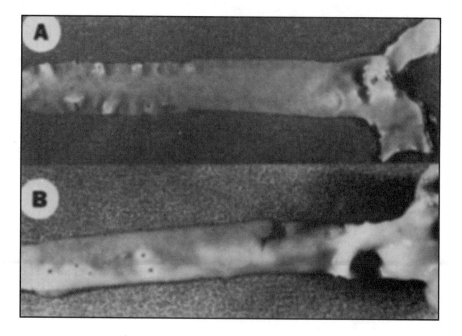

• Picture A. Animals on a diet rich in vitamin C showed no atherosclerotic deposits. Optimum collagen reinforcement protected the blood vessel walls of these animals.

• Picture B. In contrast, animals on a low vitamin C diet rapidly developed atherosclerotic deposits in their arteries (white areas). Just as in the human system, these deposits develop primarily close to the heart (white areas at right side of the picture), and around the branching regions of smaller arteries where blood flow turbulences increase the amount of vessel wall lesions. (white circles in center of the picture B).

You should keep in mind two facts from this picture: first, only one single factor in the diet made all the difference you can see between picture A and picture B - too low intake of vitamin C in the diet. Second, not something too much in the diet, like high cholesterol or high fat caused the difference between picture A and picture B. Something too little, too little intake of vitamin C made all the difference. The deposits in the picture evidently were not the result of high fat given in the diet, rather than of fat produced by the body itself in form of repair molecules which then were deposited in the vessel wall in response to a growing instability.

The striking pictures from this experiment are visible proof for our new understanding that atherosclerotic deposits are nature's 'plaster cast' to repair blood vessel walls weakened by vitamin deficiency. After we have shown that vitamin C deficiency is in fact the primary cause of cardiovascular disease it is now time to present some of the clinical evidence for the benefits of vitamins in the prevention of cardiovascular disease.

Vitamin C Cuts Heart Disease Rate in Half

"Vitamin C linked to heart benefits" was the headline in the *New York Times* on May 8, 1992. Dr. James Enstrom and his colleagues from the School of Public Health at the University of California at Los Angeles had reported a study of more than 11,000 Americans over a period of 10 years. These researchers compared the numbers of deaths from heart disease in Americans taking 300 milligrams of vitamin C per day in the form of fruits or nutritional supplements, and the heart disease rate of those taking the amount of vitamin C contained in an average American diet. The dramatic findings of this study were that in men, taking high amounts of vitamin C in their diet, the number of deaths from heart attacks, strokes and other forms of cardiovascular disease were about half that in the control group. In women who took 300 milligrams of vitamin C and more, the heart disease rate was about one-third less than in the control group.

Thus, a simple measure, the daily intake of 300 milligrams of vitamin C in the diet was associated with preventing heart attacks or strokes in every second man and in one out of three women. In few areas of medicine, more progress has been made in recent years than in the area of vitamins in the prevention of cardiovascular disease.

Study in Six European Countries Confirms:
More Vitamins - Less Heart Disease

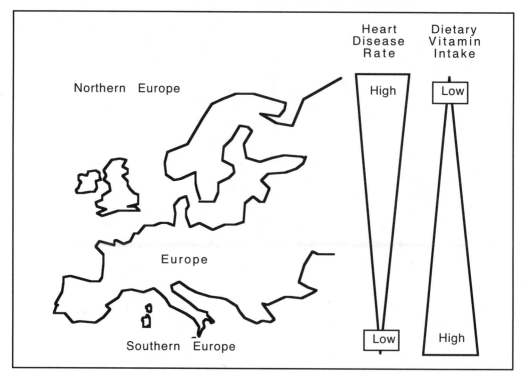

One of the largest studies ever conducted which compare the rate for heart disease with vitamin intake and vitamin concentration in the blood was carried out in thousands of patients from six European countries. The striking finding were the following:
• People living in Northern Europe had low levels of vitamins and a high rate of heart disease.
• People living in Southern Europe had high blood levels of vitamins and low incidence of heart disease.

The study also investigated cholesterol as a possible risk factor and evaluated its importance. It was found that low vitamin levels were a much greater risk factor for heart disease than high levels of cholesterol. In other words, the most important way to prevent heart disease is to watch out for an optimum intake of vitamins, in particular vitamin C, E, and beta carotene. Lowering cholesterol levels remains desirable, but it is evidently of secondary importance.

This study may finally cast some scientific light on the fact that people from France, Greece, and from other Southern European countries have a low incidence of heart disease. The explanation for this phenomenon is of course not the high consumption of wine (France) or olive oil (Greece). The answer is much simpler. The people in Southern Europe and around the Mediterranean Sea enjoy a diet high in vitamin rich fruits and vegetables.

Our New Understanding of Cardiovascular Disease

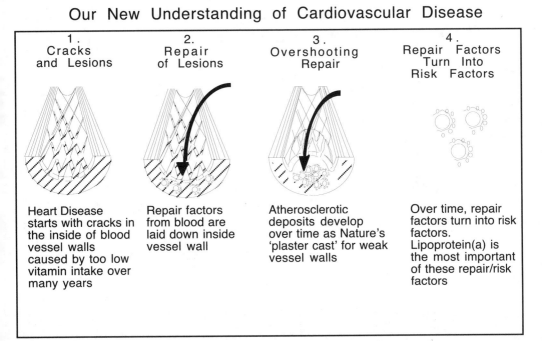

1. Cracks and Lesions	2. Repair of Lesions	3. Overshooting Repair	4. Repair Factors Turn Into Risk Factors
Heart Disease starts with cracks in the inside of blood vessel walls caused by too low vitamin intake over many years	Repair factors from blood are laid down inside vessel wall	Atherosclerotic deposits develop over time as Nature's 'plaster cast' for weak vessel walls	Over time, repair factors turn into risk factors. Lipoprotein(a) is the most important of these repair/risk factors

We have now gained a new understanding of the nature of cardiovascular disease which has direct consequences for prevention and therapy. Heart disease is not primarily the result of an abundance condition, such as a high fat diet, rather than of a deficiency condition - too low dietary intake of vitamins. The first step is the development of cracks and lesions in the inside of the weak blood vessel walls. These cracks occur primarily in the arteries of those organs with mechanical stress, like the heart which pumps constantly. With this new understanding we can suddenly also explain why we get frequently heart attacks but rarely infarctions of the nose, knee, or any other organ. The coronary arteries develop more cracks and repair due to the great mechanical stress on the coronary arteries by the pumping heart.

The second step is the attempt of the body to repair these cracks and to mend the weakened vessel wall. For this purpose cholesterol and other repair factors (=risk factors) leave the blood stream, enter the blood vessel wall through these cracks and are deposited inside the vessel wall by the thousand.

Unfortunately, with low vitamin intake over many years this initially beneficial repair mechanism overshoots. This is when the problem starts. With continued repair over years, fat molecules and other repair factors accumulate in the inside of the vessel wall. Atherosclerotic deposits develop as nature's 'plaster cast' for the weakened vessel walls.

Finally, we have a new understanding and a new definition of 'risk factors' for heart disease. Cholesterol and other 'risk factors' in our body are genuine 'repair factors'. Only if the repair process at the blood vessel wall continues for too long will these 'repair factors' turn into 'risk factors'. Let us now have a closer look at the most important of these risk factors, lipoprotein(a). This new risk factor will lead us to further therapeutic breakthroughs in the treatment of cardiovascular disease.

Cholesterol, Low-Density Lipoprotein (LDL) and Lipoprotein(a)

For half a century it was thought that cholesterol is the main factor leading to the buildup of deposits. More recently, LDL cholesterol was proposed to be the villain for the development of atherosclerotic deposits. Today we know that these factors play only a secondary role. Atherosclerotic deposits are essentially the result of the newly identified risk factor lipoprotein(a). This figure explains what cholesterol, low density lipoprotein (LDL) and lipoprotein(a) have in common and what sets them apart.

Cholesterol. Cholesterol is a very important molecule for the growth of every cell in our bodies. Cholesterol molecules do not swim in the blood like fat in the soup. Thousands of cholesterol molecules are packed together with other fat molecules in tiny round globules called lipoproteins. Millions of these fat-transporting vehicles circulate in our body at any time. The best-known among these are high density lipoproteins (HDL, or "good cholesterol") and low density lipoprotein (LDL, or "bad cholesterol").

LDL Cholesterol . Most of the cholesterol molecules in the blood are transported in millions of LDL particles in the blood. By carrying cholesterol and other fat molecules to our body cells, LDL is a very useful transport vehicle for nutrients supplied to these cells. LDL has been named the "bad cholesterol" during the years when researchers failed to look for the real villain — the "very bad cholesterol" — which causes blood vessel deposits: lipoprotein(a).

Lipoprotein(a) . Lipoprotein(a) is an LDL particle plus an additional adhesive protein wrapped around it. This biological adhesive tape is named apoprotein(a), or apo(a). It makes the lipoprotein(a) fat globule one of the stickiest particles in our body. In brief, lipoprotein(a) is a sticky fat globule and because of these properties it is a primary risk factor for cardiovascular disease. The adhesive apo(a) is responsible for millions of lipoprotein(a) fat globules sticking inside the walls of the blood vessels and forming atherosclerotic deposits. In contrast, LDL has no adhesive tape and therefore is much less of a risk factor. Less adhesive — less risk for heart disease. Further details are presented in *Eradicating Heart Disease.*

There is now an overwhelming amount of evidence from clinical studies and from direct analysis of the blood vessel wall that lipoprotein(a) is the primary risk factor for heart attacks, strokes, the clogging of bypass vessels after coronary bypass surgery and for the clogging after angioplasty. A recent re-evaluation of the Framingham Heart Study, the largest heart risk factor study ever conducted, showed that lipoprotein(a) is a ten times greater risk factor for heart disease than total cholesterol or LDL cholesterol.

Nature's Top Blood Vessel Repair Molecule Becomes Greatest Risk Factor for Heart Disease

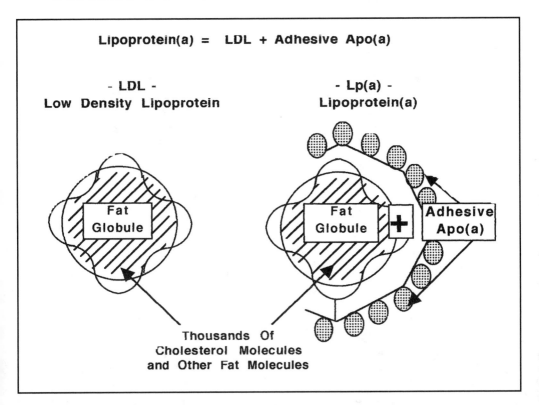

Lipoprotein(a) = LDL + Adhesive Apo(a)

- LDL -
Low Density Lipoprotein

- Lp(a) -
Lipoprotein(a)

Fat Globule

Fat Globule **+** Adhesive Apo(a)

Thousands Of Cholesterol Molecules and Other Fat Molecules

The question is legitimate: Why would nature produce a molecule that kills millions of people by accumulating in the walls of the arteries and by causing heart attacks? The answer is strikingly simple: There has to be an advantage to lipoprotein(a), to its stickiness, to its cholesterol transport, etc. We know already what this advantage is: repair! Lipoprotein(a) is nature's top repair molecule. Only if this repair goes on for too long will this repair molecule turn into a risk factor, and only then will the advantage turn into a disadvantage. It's so simple and logical!

You may also ask: If lipoprotein(a) can really become a ten times greater risk factor for heart disease than cholesterol or LDL-cholesterol, why haven't I read about it in the newspaper or seen it on TV? Again the answer is simple. Currently, no pharmaceutical company has a treatment available to reduce the risk from lipoprotein(a). Consequently, there is no budget available from anywhere to inform and to educate millions of people about this new risk factor. Moreover, cholesterol-lowering drugs are best-sellers among prescription drugs.

Based on an irrefutable amount of clinical data, lipoprotein(a) is the primary risk factor for heart disease known today. I believe that there is every reason to talk about it. Even more so, since on the next pages you will learn about an effective natural therapy to reduce the risk from lipoprotein(a), or Lp(a).

The World's First Therapy to Reverse Heart Disease Naturally — Without Surgery

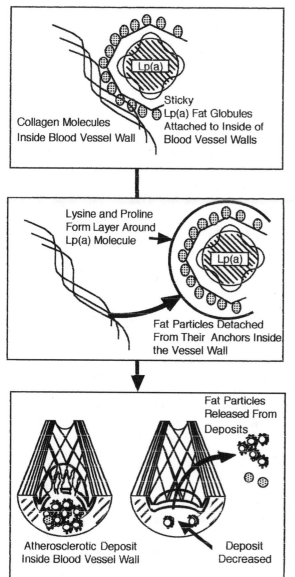

Collagen Molecules Inside Blood Vessel Wall

Sticky Lp(a) Fat Globules Attached to Inside of Blood Vessel Walls

Lysine and Proline Form Layer Around Lp(a) Molecule

Fat Particles Detached From Their Anchors Inside the Vessel Wall

Fat Particles Released From Deposits

Atherosclerotic Deposit Inside Blood Vessel Wall

Deposit Decreased

Many Lp(a) fat globules have entered the weakened blood vessel wall. Thousands of them are attached to collagen and other structures inside the walls of blood vessels. Once attached, they can also bind other fat globules, like LDL.

The stickiness of the fat globules became another important aspect of our new understanding of the development of atherosclerotic deposits.

Consequently, therapeutic agents which can neutralize this stickiness had to be found — "teflon" agents for the vessel wall.

The first generation of these blood vessel teflon agents are the natural amino acids lysine and proline. Lysine and proline form a protective layer around the sticky Lp(a) fat globule.

Lysine and proline have two main effects:
• Preventing the attachment of further Lp(a) and other fat globules inside the blood vessel wall.
• Releasing already deposited Lp(a) and other fat globules from atherosclerotic deposits.

The release of thousands of previously deposited fat globules from the blood vessel wall decreases the size of the atherosclerotic deposits and thereby reverses existing heart disease.

The fat globules are released gradually, they enter the bloodstream and subsequently they are burned in the liver. This a a natural form of treatment and there is no risk for complications as it is the case for angioplasty treatment or other surgical treatments.

The First Patented Therapy
to Reverse Heart Disease Without Surgery

The Commissioner of Patents and Trademarks

Has received an application for a patent for a new and useful invention. The title and description of the invention are enclosed. The requirements of law have been complied with, and it has been determined that a patent on the invention shall be granted under the law.

Therefore, this

United States Patent

Grants to the person or persons having title to this patent the right to exclude others from making, using or selling the invention throughout the United States of America for the term of seventeen years from the date of this patent, subject to the payment of maintenance fees as provided by law.

Commissioner of Patents and Trademarks

Attest

With the possibility to reverse existing heart disease in a natural way — without angioplasty or bypass surgery — an old dream of mankind has come true. I am aware that this medical breakthrough sounds almost to good to be true. Even more important is the fact that the U.S. Patent Office has reviewed the available scientific evidence and has approved the use of lysine, synthetic lysine analogs and vitamin C for the prevention and the reversal of atherosclerotic deposits and of cardiovascular disease.

It is an ironic side aspect that the U.S. Patent Office, a federal agency, acknowledges the potential value of vitamins and other essential nutrients for the treatment of heart disease at a time when another federal agency, the U.S. Food and Drug Administration, FDA, tries to limit access to nutritional supplements by making them prescription drugs.

These patents are also a personal reward for the scientific drive toward this breakthrough which I have led over the past decade, as well as for all my colleagues involved. Further details on this new therapeutic technology are summarized in *Eradicating Heart Disease*.

The Cellular Essential Program

Introduction to the Cellular Essential Program

In the first part of this book I have taken you on a journey through the human body and its cardiovascular system. We have seen that:

- Cardiovascular disease starts with an instability of the vessel wall caused by vitamin deficiency,
- Atherosclerotic deposits are nothing else than nature's "plaster cast" to make up for this instability,
- Lipoprotein(a) is nature's top repair molecule, and this repair molecule turns into a risk factor during chronic vitamin deficiency.
- We have seen an old dream of mankind come true: the exciting possibility to reverse cardiovascular disease naturally — without angioplasty or bypass surgery.
- We have seen in large-scale clinical studies that if blood levels of vitamin C and other antioxidant vitamins are high, the rate of cardiovascular disease is low.
- We also concluded that lowering blood levels of cholesterol and other risk factors remain desirable, although it is no longer the primary aim.

But our journey through the human body has only just begun. In the second part of this book we will make an exciting visit to the cells, the small units which make up our body and our cardiovascular system. In particular, we will see that:

- The heart and the cardiovascular system is built of millions of cells.
- These cells function like small factories.
- These cell factories need cell fuel and energy to function properly.
- Vitamins and other cellular essentials are the basis of cell life.
- Health and disease of our body is determined on the level of cells.

Most importantly, you will be introduced to a daily program of cellular essentials which is scientifically formulated to optimize your cardiovascular health. By following this program you can take immediate advantage of everything you are reading in this book. Before we have a closer look at these cellular essentials, let us define the essentials of life.

Life Essentials

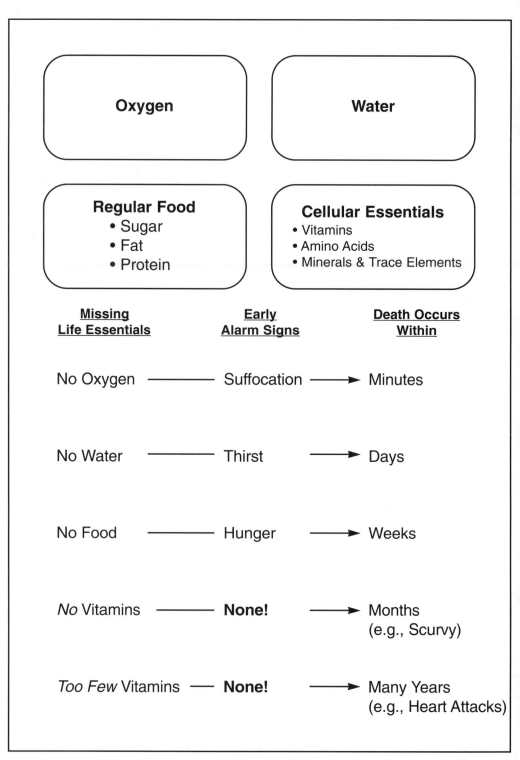

Cellular Essentials Are Part of *Life* Essentials

The term "Cellular Essentials" is defined here as all those substances our body cells need to function properly but hardly ever get in the regular diet. Cellular essentials primarily comprise vitamins, certain amino acids, minerals and trace elements.

As we can see from the adjacent figure, cellular essentials are an important part of life essentials. These life essentials comprise very familiar things like oxygen from the air, water, regular food, but also — cellular essentials. The figure will help you to become aware of the fact that vitamins and other cellular essentials are a basic part of life and of your body's health. To be aware of the basic character of cellular essentials for the health of your body and of your cardiovascular system is the key for this program.

Something else is noteworthy in the figure. Lack of oxygen, lack of water and lack of food all give us alarm signs in the form of suffocation, thirst and hunger. Cellular essentials are the only group of life essentials that does not give us alarm signs if they are deficient. This fact has dramatic consequences for our health. It means that our body does not tell us automatically if we are deficient in cellular essentials. The first sign of a deficiency in cellular essentials is the outbreak of the diseases *itself*. A total lack of cellular essentials can lead to disease and death within several months, such as in scurvy. Since we all get small amounts of vitamins and other cellular essentials, we generally do not suffer from a total depletion.

Most of us, however, suffer from a chronic deficiency in vitamins and other cellular essentials. These deficiencies also don't have alarm signs and they can continue unrecognized and masked over many years. In most cases the first sign of chronic vitamin deficiency is a heart attack or the outbreak of another disease which has silently developed over many years.

The bottom line of this is: Since our body does not give us alarm signs about deficiencies in cellular essentials, the only way we can avoid them is to use our minds and to make ourselves aware of the importance of a daily supplementation with these cellular essentials. That is the purpose of this book.

Cellular Health Determines Body Health

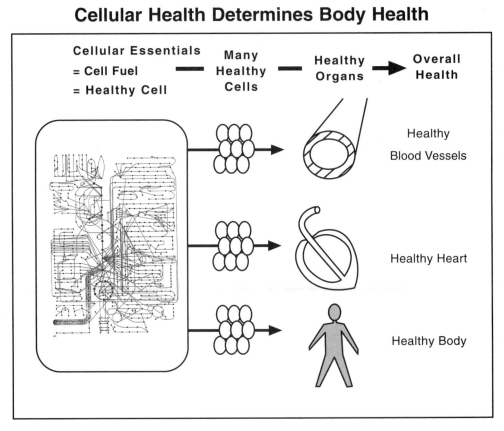

Our body is made up of billions of cells. Each cell works like a factory, fulfilling many different functions. The cells of the blood vessels have different functions from the heart cells. And even the cells of the heart have different functions such as pumping and conducting electricity for the heartbeat. Like a real factory a cell needs raw material (food), and cell fuel (cellular essentials).

But how does a cell know what to do? Amazingly, each cell in our body contains a biological software program. This software program contains all the information for the "production assembly line" in this cell. The figure above shows you schematically such a software program. The figure is taken from *Cell,* one of the most widely read scientific textbooks. Each oval shape is a different molecule (product). The lines connecting the molecules indicate a biological reaction, or a step in the cellular assembly line. These biological reactions need catalysts. As we will see, vitamins and other cellular essentials are the most important cellular catalysts we know. We therefore can use the terms catalysts, cell fuel or cellular essentials synonymously.

The figure shows that health and disease in our arteries, our hearts and in any other organ of our body ultimately depends on cellular health. Optimum supply with cellular essentials is a cornerstone for optimum health of our body and its organs.

Cellular Essentials as Cell Energy Carriers

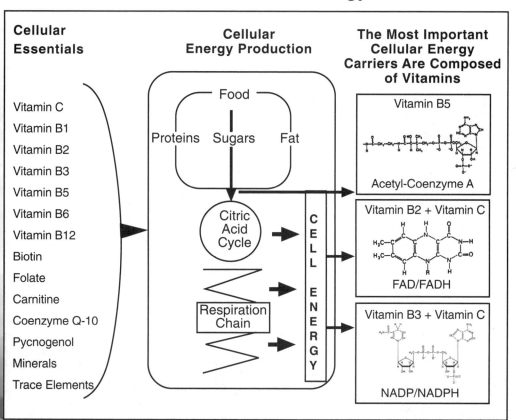

Besides their role as catalysts in the cell production assembly line, cellular essentials have another important function: they are carriers of cellular energy. Just like in our daily life, our body has to accomplish the task to create, transport and regenerate energy. This is not an obscure mechanism. Important steps of this energy process in each cell have been scientifically elucidated. The above figure gives you some insight in the form of a schematic overview. Together with the breakdown products of regular food (proteins, sugars, fats), cellular essentials are part of the metabolism of each cell in our cardiovascular system and our body in general. The most important carrier molecules for cellular energy are composed of vitamins:

  • Vitamin B3 (Niacin) is the carrier molecule for the cell energy carrier NADP. Vitamin C is needed to charge or recharge this molecule with cellular energy to become NADPH, a mechanism which I was privileged to identify.
  • Another important energy carrier molecule is FAD. In this case vitamin C recharges a carrier molecule made up of vitamin B2 (Flavin).

Science, biology and medical students around the world are familiar with these energy carrier molecules. Unfortunately, this important knowledge is not put to work in medical practice yet. The program in this book will help to change this situation. Everyone can now understand the principles of cellular essentials and can immediately benefit from this knowledge.

Cellular Essentials and the Cardiovascular System

Millions of cells make up our heart, the walls for the blood vessels all other parts of the cardiovascular system. Moreover, millions of cells circulate in the bloodstream. Each of these cells has a precisely defined function.

The picture at left shows red blood cells responsible for oxygen transport and white blood cells which function as the body's "phone cells," e.g. in the defense against free radicals.

The picture at right shows platelets which are responsible for blood clotting during wound healing and repair.

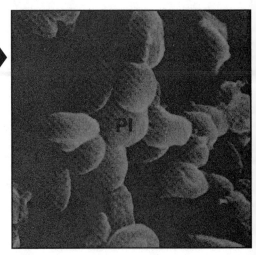

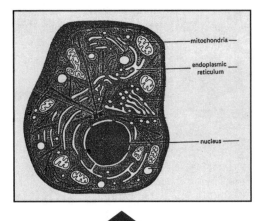

Each cell is a **factory.** The core (nucleus) contains the information (software) for the cell function. Each cell also contains power plants (mitochondria) and production assembly lines (endoplasmic reticulum).

The **software program** in each cell determines each step in the production assembly line of the cell's life. This software program varies according to the different tasks of each cell and each organ.

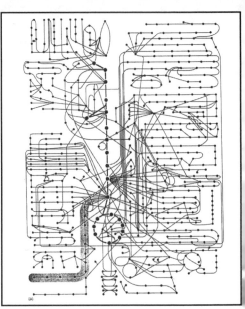

Deficiencies in Cellular Essentials Can Cause or Aggravate Different Forms of Heart Disease

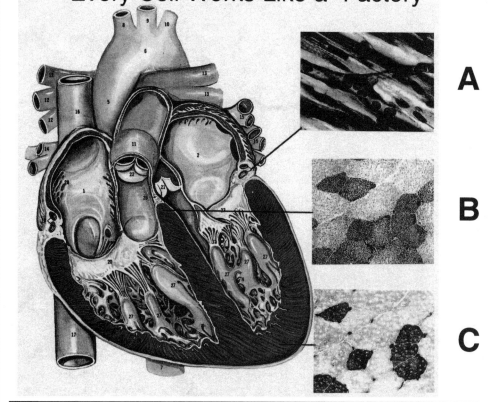

Millions of Cells Make Up the Heart
Every Cell Works Like a "Factory"

Deficiency of Cellular Essentials In	Can Cause or Worsen the Following Condition	What You Could Get
A: Cells in Coronary Artery Walls	Development of Atherosclerotic Deposits	Angina Pectoris Heart Attack
B: Heart Cells (Electricity)	Impaired Conduction of Heart Electricty	Irregular Heartbeat (Arrhythmia)
C: Heart Cells (Pumping)	Insufficient Blood Pumping	Shortness of Breath Edema, Severe Fatigue

Cellular Essentials Contribute to a Healthy Heart

Let us now have a close look at the heart, the most important and mechanically the most active organ in our body. It pumps 70 times a minute and 100,000 times a day. The importance of an optimum supply of cellular essentials for this busy organ is obvious. The heart in our body has been compared to the motor in a car: both need special care and fuel.

The adjacent figure shows that the entire heart is made up of cells.
• **A:** We already know about the coronary arteries, the blood supply pipeline of the heart. Besides the connective tissue (collagen, etc.), the wall of these coronary arteries is made up of cells. One of the important functions of cells in the wall of arteries is to form a barrier lining that separates the bloodstream from the blood vessel wall itself. If these cells (endothelial cells) are impaired, risk factors from the blood can easily enter the blood vessel wall and lead to deposits. Cellular essentials help to keep this cell barrier intact and thereby protect the entire vessel wall from damage.

• **B:** The heart itself is essentially composed of muscle cells. A small portion of these cells has the fascinating ability to create and to conduct electricity needed for the heartbeat. If these electrical cells lack cellular essentials, their ability to create and to conduct electricity is impaired. These are the patients who develop irregular heartbeat (arrhythmia) or in whom already irregular heartbeat worsens. The remedy is strikingly simple. Resupplementing your diet with cellular essentials will optimize the function of your electrical heart cells and will help normalize your heartbeat.

• **C:** The largest portion of the heart cells have the task to pump the blood out into the circulation. Thus the task of these muscle cells is to contract with every heartbeat like the members of a multi-million player orchestra. Lack of cellular essentials in millions of heart muscle cells leads to insufficient contraction and to insufficient blood pumping. Instead of one teacup of blood that is pumped under healthy conditions, an impaired heart pumps perhaps half a teacup of blood into the circulation. These are the patients with shortness of breath, edema, and with severe fatigue. Again, in most cases the remedy is strikingly simple. Resupplement cellular essentials in your diet to optimize the function of millions of heart muscle cells.

There are, of course, certain conditions (e.g., after a heart attack when millions of heart muscle cells have died off), when resupplementing cellular essentials cannot restore total health. In general, however, you will be surprised how greatly you can benefit from supplementing your diet with cellular essentials. If you are on any prescription medication, please continue this medication and add the cellular essential program to it. Do not stop taking your regular medication without consulting your physician.

For those among my readers who are healthy and do not suffer from any heart condition, the perspective is even more encouraging. By resupplementing cellular essentials in your diet you can help *prevent* the development of heart conditions in the first place. "An ounce of prevention is worth a pound of cure."

On the following pages I will introduce you to the cellular essential program which I recommend for everyone, young and old, to optimize cardiovascular performance and health.

Cardiovascular Cellular Essentials

The following nutritional program is scientifically formulated to protect your cardiovascular system and to optimize its health. It contains all the vitamins, amino acids and minerals of my 10 Step Program for Optimum Cardiovascular Health. The recommendations listed below are the minimum daily recommendations for adolescents and adults to maintain optimum cardiovascular health.

VITAMINS

Vitamin C		300 mg
(from Ascorbic Acid	200 mg	
from Ascorbyl Palmitate	100 mg)	
Vitamin E (d-Alpha Tocopherol)		200 I.U.
Vitamin A (Beta-Carotene)		2,500 I.U.
Vitamin B1 (Thiamine)		10 mg
Vitamin B2 (Riboflavin)		10 mg
Vitamin B3		
(from Niacin	15 mg	
from Niacinamide	50 mg)	
Vitamin B5 (Pantothenate)		60 mg
Vitamin B6 (Pyridoxine)		15 mg
Vitamin B12 (Cyanocobalamin)		30 mcg
Vitamin D		200 I.U.
Folic Acid		130 mg
Biotin		100 mcg

MINERALS

Calcium	50 mg
Magnesium	60 mg
Potassium	30 mg
Phosphate	20 mg
Zinc	10 mg
Manganese	2 mg
Copper	500 mcg
Selenium	30 mcg
Chromium	15 mcg
Molybdenum	6 mcg

OTHER IMPORTANT NUTRIENTS

L-Proline	150 mg
L-Lysine	150 mg
L-Carnitine	50 mg
L-Arginine	50 mg
L-Cysteine	50 mg
Inositol	50 mg
Coenzyme Q-10	10 mg
Pycnogenol	10 mg

How to Take Cardiovascular Essentials

- The above formula of cardiovascular essentials is a daily program everyone can and should follow who is interested in maintaining optimum cardiovascular health.
- This daily formula is safe for everyone to take - from age 20 to 100.
- Patients with existing heart conditions may double or triple this formula. If you are a patient do not stop taking your regular medication. Add the nutritional supplement program and consult with your doctor.
- Cardiovascular essentials are best taken in the morning and in the evening with meals in order to enhance their absorption.

Vitamin C Formula

The individual requirement for vitamin C varies more than for any other vitamin
- from one person to another
- within the same person between a healthy condition, stress conditions, and diseases.

I therefore developed a special vitamin C formula to allow adaptation to your personal requirement. The composition of different forms of vitamin C is particularly valuable because,

- it contains vitamin C salts with enhanced biological availability,
- it contains vitamin C- plamitate (ascorbyl-palmitate), a fat-soluble form of vitamin C which is taken up by cells at a much higher rate than regular vitamin C,
- it contains bioflavonoids which work synergistically with vitamin C and increase its biological efficacy in our body,
- it is well digested even if you take several tablets a day.

An adult person may take 1-5 tablets of vitamin C per day. Persons with an existing heart condition may take up to 8 or 10 tablets of vitamin C per day. Moreover, persons with an increased risk for heart disease, such as diabetic patients, may also have to take higher amounts. These tablets should be taken in split dosages to maximize absorption, as vitamin C is water soluble. For further details please read the respective chapters in Eradicating Heart Disease.

One tablet of this Vitamin C Formula contains:

Ascorbic Acid	150 mg
Ascorbyl Palmitate	150 mg
Calcium Ascorbate	150 mg
Magnesium Ascorbate	150 mg
Bioflavonoids	150 mg

The Power of the Cellular Essentials Program

The real power of this cellular essentials program becomes obvious if we have a close look at the different ingredients and what medical science tells us about their importance for our health.

Vitamin C
- Vitamin C is the key cellular essential for the stability of our blood vessels, our heart and all other organs of our body. Without vitamin C our body would literally collapse and dissolve, as it happens in scurvy.
- Vitamin C is responsible for an optimum production and function of collagen, elastin and other connective tissue molecules which give stability to the blood vessel walls and to our body.
- Vitamin C is important for fast wound healing throughout our body, including the healing of millions of tiny wounds and lesions inside of our blood vessel walls.
- Vitamin C is the most important antioxidant of the body. Optimum amounts of vitamin C protect the cardiovascular system and the body effectively against biological rusting.
- Vitamin C is also a cofactor for a series of biological catalysts (enzymes) which are important for an improved metabolism of cholesterol, triglycerides and other risk factors, which helps to decrease the risk for cardiovascular disease.
- Vitamin C is an important energy molecule to recharge energy carriers inside the cells.

Vitamin E
- Vitamin E is the most important fat-soluble antioxidant vitamin. It protects particularly the membranes of the cells in our cardiovascular system and our body against attacks from free radicals and against oxidative damage.
- Vitamin E is enriched in low-density lipoproteins (LDL) and other cholesterol and fat transporting particles. Taken in optimum amounts, vitamin E can prevent these fat particles from oxidation (biological rusting) and from damaging the inside of the blood vessel walls.
- Vitamin E was shown to render the platelets in our blood circulation less sticky, thereby keeping our blood "thin" and decreasing the risk from blood clotting.

Beta-Carotene
- Beta-Carotene is also called pro-vitamin A and is another important fat-soluble antioxidant vitamin. Like vitamin E, it is transported primarily in lipoprotein particles in our bloodstream to millions of body cells. Like vitamin E, beta-carotene protects these fat particles from rusting and from becoming damaging to the cardiovascular system. Considering these scientific facts, it is not surprising that vitamin C, vitamin E, and beta-carotene are documented in a rapidly growing number of clinical studies as powerful protecting agents against cardiovascular disease.
- Similar to vitamin E, beta-carotene has been shown to decrease the risk from blood clotting.

Vitamin B1 (Thiamine)
- A cellular essential which functions as the cofactor for an important catalyst called pyrophosphate. This catalyst is involved in phosphate metabolism in our cells, another key energy source to optimize millions of reactions in our cardiovascular cells and our body.

Vitamin B2 (Riboflavin)
- Riboflavin is the cofactor for flavin adenosin dinucleotide (FAD), one of the most important carrier molecules of cellular energy inside the tiny energy centers (power plants) of all cells.

Vitamin B3 (Niacin, Niacinamide)
- Niacin is an important cellular essential as the cofactor for nicotinamide adenosin dinucleotide phosphate (NADP), and related energy carrier molecules. This energy carrier molecule is one of the most important energy transport systems in our entire body. Millions of these carriers are created and recharged (by vitamin C) inside the cellular energy centers of our cardiovascular system and our body. Cell life and life in general would not be possible without this energy carrier.

Vitamin B5 (Pantothenate)
- Pantothenate is the cofactor for coenzyme A, the central fuel molecule in the metabolism of our heart cells our blood vessel cells and all other cells. The metabolism of carbohydrates, proteins and fats inside each cell all lead into one single molecule, acetyl coenzyme A. This molecule is the key molecule that helps to convert all food into cell energy. This important molecule is actually composed in part of vitamin B5 and the importance of supplementing this vitamin is evident. Again, cell life would not be possible without this vitamin.

Vitamin B6 (Pyridoxine)
- Vitamin B6 is the cofactor for pyridoxal phosphate, an important cofactor for the metabolism of amino acids and proteins in our cardiovascular cells and our body.
- Vitamin B6 is needed in the production of red blood cells, the carriers of oxygen to the cells of our cardiovascular system and all other cells of our body.

Vitamin B12
- Vitamin B12 is a cellular essential needed for a proper metabolism of fatty acids and certain amino acids in the cells of our body.
- Vitamin B12 is needed for the production of red blood cells. A severe deficiency of vitamin B12 can cause a disease called pernicious anemia which is characterized by an insufficient production of blood cells.

Folate
- Also a very important essential for the production of red blood cells and for oxygen supply.
- The last three vitamins are good examples how cellular essentials work together like an orchestra. Without proper oxygen transport to all the cells, their function would be impaired no matter how much of the other vitamins you take. It is therefore important to supplement your diet as completely as possible with the right cellular essentials in the right amounts.

Biotin
- Biotin is a cellular essential needed in the metabolism of carbohydrates, fats and proteins.

Inositol
- Inositol is a key cellular essential in sugar and fat metabolism in our cardiovascular cells and our body.
- Inositol is also important for the biological communication process in our body. Inositol is part of the signal communication *inside* the cells. Hormones, such as insulin, and other molecules are signals from *outside* the cell. If a hormone docks to a cell it wishes to give information to this cell. Inositol is part of the proper "reading" mechanism of this information through the cell membrane. Thus, inositol is part of the proper communication process which, in turn, is critical for optimum cardiovascular health.

Minerals
- Minerals are important cellular essentials. Calcium, magnesium and potassium are the most important among them. Minerals are needed for a multitude of catalytic reactions in each cell of our body every second of our life.

Calcium
- Calcium is an important cellular essential for the proper contraction of muscle cells including millions of heart muscle cells.
- Calcium is needed for the conduction of nerve impulses and therefore for optimum heartbeat
- Calcium is also needed for the proper biological "communication" among the cells of the cardiovascular system and most other cells, as well as for many other biological functions.

Magnesium
- Magnesium is nature's calcium antagonist and its benefit for the cardiovascular system is similar to the calcium antagonists that are prescribed; except, magnesium is produced by nature itself.
- Clinical studies have shown that magnesium is particularly important for helping to normalize elevated blood pressure; moreover, it can help normalize irregular heartbeat.

Trace Elements
- The trace elements Zinc, Manganese, Copper, Selenium, Chromium and Molybdenum are also important cellular essentials. Most of them are metals needed as catalysts for thousands of reactions in the metabolism of cells. They are needed only in very tiny amounts, less than a tenth of a thousandth of a gram. Selenium is also a very important antioxidant.

Amino Acids:

- Amino acids are the building blocks of proteins. Most of these amino acids in our body derive from regular food and from the breakdown of its protein content. Many amino acids can be synthesized by our own body when needed; these amino acids are called non-essential amino acids. Those amino acids which the body cannot synthesize are called essential amino acids.

- We need an optimum amount of essential amino acids to maintain optimum health. Interestingly, there is now important scientific evidence that even though the body can produce certain amino acids, the amount produced may not be enough to maintain proper health. A good example is the amino acid proline.

Proline

- The amino acid proline is a major building block of the stability proteins collagen and elastin which we already know. One-fourth to one-third of the reinforcement collagen rods, for example, is made up of proline. It is easy to understand how important it is for the optimum stability of our blood vessels and our body in general to get an optimum amount of proline in our diet.

- Proline is also very important in reversing atherosclerotic deposits. As we have seen earlier in this book, cholesterol-carrying fat globules(lipoproteins) are attached to the inside of the blood vessel wall via biological "adhesive tapes." Proline is a formidable "teflon" agent which can neutralize the stickiness of these fat globules. The potential therapeutic effect is two-fold; first, proline helps to prevent the further buildup of atherosclerotic deposits and, second, proline helps to release already deposited fat globules from the blood vessel wall into the bloodstream. When many fat globules are released from the blood vessel deposits, its size decreases leading to a reversal of cardiovascular disease.

- We have patents pending for the use of proline alone and in combination with other essential nutrients in the reversal of heart disease.

- Proline can be synthesized by the body, but the amounts synthesized are frequently too little, particularly in patients with an increased risk for cardiovascular disease.

Lysine

- As opposed to proline, lysine is an essential amino acid, which means that the body cannot synthesize this amino acid at all. A daily supplementation of this amino acid is therefore critical. Lysine, like proline, is enriched in collagen and the other stability molecules and its intake helps to stabilize the blood vessels and the other organs in the body.

- In addition, lysine is another "teflon" agent which can help release deposited fat globules from the blood vessel deposits. People with existing cardiovascular disease may increase their daily intake of lysine and proline to several grams, in addition to the basic program recommended in this book.

- Both lysine and proline benefit from a combined intake of vitamin C. In order to properly function in the collagen molecules and in the other stability molecules, the amino acids lysine and proline need to be chemically modified into hydroxy-lysine and hydroxy-proline. This is accomplished by vitamin C, nature's most effective "hydroxylating" agent.
- We have been issued patents for the use of lysine and synthetic lysine analogs, particularly in combination with vitamin C, for the prevention and treatment of cardiovascular disease. These patents are the world's first patents for a therapy to reverse heart disease — without surgery.

Arginine

- Arginine has many functions in the human body. In connection with the cardiovascular system, one function is of particular importance. The amino acid arginine can split off a small molecule called nitric oxide. This tiny part of the former arginine molecule has a powerful role in maintaining cardiovascular health. Nitric oxide relaxes the blood vessel walls and thereby helps to normalize high blood pressure. In addition, nitric oxide helps to decrease the stickiness of platelets and thereby has an anti-clogging effect.

Cysteine

- Cysteine is another important amino acid with many important functions in our body. The cardiovascular system benefits particularly from a supplementation with this amino acid because cysteine is a building block of glutathione, one of the most important antioxidants produced in the body. Among others, glutathione protects the inside of the blood vessel walls from free radical and other damage.

Carnitine

- Carnitine is an extremely important amino acid and cellular essential. It is needed for the proper conversion of fat into energy. Carnitine functions like a "shuttle" between the cell factory and the energy compartment within each cell. It transports energy molecules in and out of these cellular power plants. This mechanism is particularly important for all muscle cells, including those of the heart. For the constantly pumping heart muscle, carnitine is one of the most critical cell fuels. Thus, it is not surprising that many clinical studies have documented the great value of carnitine supplementation in improving the pumping function and the performance of the heart.
- Carnitine also benefits the electrical cells of the heart and its supplementation has been shown to help normalize different forms of irregular heartbeat.

Coenzyme Q-10

- Coenzyme Q-10 is a very important cellular essential. It is also known as ubiquinone. Coenzyme Q-10 functions as an extremely important catalyst inside the energy center of each cell.
- Because of its high workload, the heart muscle cells have a particularly high demand of Coenzyme Q-10. In patients with insufficient pumping function of the heart, this cellular essential is frequently deficient. An irrefutable number of clinical studies has documented

the great value of Coenzyme Q-10 in the treatment of heart failure and for optimum heart performance.

Pycnogenol

- Pycnogenol is the name for a group of bioflavonoids (proanthocyanidins) with remarkable properties. In the cardiovascular system pycnogenol has several important functions:
- Pycnogenols are powerful antioxidants which work together with vitamin C and vitamin E in the defense of free radical damage to the cardiovascular system.
- Together with vitamin C, pycnogenols have a particular value in stabilizing the blood vessel walls including the capillaries. Pycnogenols have been shown to bind to elastin (after collagen, the most important stability molecule), and protect elastin molecules against attacking enzymes.
- It is therefore not surprising that pycnogenols have been shown to reduce capillary bleeding and other forms of capillary leakage such as edema.

For some of my readers the description of the different effects of the cellular essentials may seem rather technical. I chose this language on purpose. The results you will see from following this program are so amazing that you will be asked many questions. "How can that be?" Rather than burdening you with the answer, let this book speak.

There are no miracles or magicians at work. Every single ingredient is scientifically based and the health improvements can be experienced from now on by anyone, anywhere in the world. I consider it my responsibility to provide my readers with the best and most accurate information there is about this cellular essential program.

This Cellular Essentials Program is the best scientifically based, natural protection there is for anyone from age 20 to 100 who is looking forward to a long and healthy life. You should never forget, your body is as old as your blood vessels. The care you take of your cardiovascular system now will pay back manifold throughout your life.

On the following pages I will share with you some of the letters grateful patients who have been following my nutritional cardiovascular program wrote to me .

Testimonials from Patients With Angina Pectoris
Who Are Following my Cardiovascular Program

Dear Dr. Rath:

In May, 1992 some extraordinary physical exertion on my part brought on pain that was especially noticeable in my left arm and left shoulder. I thought that I had badly strained these muscles in my upper body. There was so much discomfort that I was not able to sleep until the morning hours. By the next morning the pain had progressed to the middle of my chest and I then recognized the pain as angina.

Immediately, I started a series of treatments. During the treatments and after, I started a walking program. Although my walking did not cause any severe angina pain, there was still a tightness in my chest and a necessity to slow down my pace because of a shortness of breath.

It wasn't until I started following your cardiovascular health recommendations that I experienced a difference. Remarkably, within a month the discomfort from walking had entirely disappeared.

Presently, I am walking 2.5 miles at least 3 days per week at a very fast clip with no discomfort whatsoever. I am cognizant that the buildup within my blood vessel walls occurred over a long time period, so I am prepared to continue following your recommendations on a continuous basis. It's a small price to pay for arteries that are free of atherosclerotic deposits.

Thanks for your cardiovascular recommendations! I feel that you have made a tremendous scientific breakthrough in the treatment of heart disease.

M.L., USA

Dear Dr. Rath:

I had been having chest pain (angina pectoris) for several years on the average of about every three weeks. Since I started to follow your cardiovascular health recommendations over 90 days ago, I have only had chest pain one time, which was about three weeks after receiving my first bottle.

I am following your cardiovascular health recommendations because I feel that proper nutrition can prevent eighty percent of our health problems.

E.T., USA

Dear Dr. Rath:

I have asthma, controlled high blood pressure and angina. After following your recommendations for cardiovascular health I feel wonderful — I feel like I have more energy and can do my work easier — no chest pain, coughing or leg pains. My whole body feels light, as if I lost weight. It is a very good feeling.

Thank you for helping us in our older years.

Sincerely,

The B's

From a patient's letter to his doctor:

I can't wait to see you in six weeks. Since following Dr. Rath's cardiovascular health recommendations I have had no angina. This past May I walked and climbed the rugged ocean trails of the rain forest without so much as a twinge. And recently, I have walked the last 2-18 holes of golf — something unheard of since my heart attack.

In closing, I and my family are very pleased and would like to thank you.

J.T., Canada

Do YOU have a similar experience? Send your letter to Dr. Rath. Your confidential letter on your health improvements can help thousands of other readers in the future to make the right decision. They will thank you!

Testimonials from Patients With Irregular Heartbeat Following my Cardiovascular Program

Dear Dr. Rath:

Two months ago, I was experiencing loud heartbeats, tachycardia and irregular beating of the heart. I saw my doctor who promptly put me on antiarrhythmic medication. I can honestly say this medication did me absolutely no good.

Because I've tried to investigate alternative treatments for my ailments (I've had diabetes for 38 years), I began to follow your recommendations for cardiovascular health. What a smart decision that was! Within a few days, the tachycardia stopped and I've not experienced any loud or irregular heartbeats. It's like a miracle. It must be the combination of nutrients you suggest because I had been taking Coenzyme Q10 separately from my regular vitamins. I tell everyone I know about the benefits of your cardiovascular recommendations and mention it during the diabetic seminars that I am conducting. At the last seminar I handed out copies of your letter, with a list of the ingredients in your recommendations. I hope you won't mind.

Because of your research, I'm able to continue working.

B.M., USA

Dear Dr. Rath,

How delightful, after following your cardiovascular health recommendations for just 2 months, one notices the absence of irregular heartbeats, and the freedom to breathe freely. Confidence is restored as one has increased vigor and endurance. In a word, one spends less time thinking about their heart and more time enjoying life.

All this by simply following your cardiovascular health recommendations, which have become the answer for resolving coronary problems.

I am happy to have this opportunity of expressing my gratitude for your advanced medical research and for your cardiovascular health recommendations .

J.S., USA

Testimonials from Patients with Heart Failure (Impaired Heart Performance) Who Are Following my Cardiovascular Program

Dear Dr. Rath:

I am happy to report that your cardiovascular health recommendations have improved my life! Now I can climb the stairs readily and without shortness of breath. I can also resume hiking for 3-4 miles a day without feeling tired and exhausted. I do have an energetic outlook toward life and I'm sure it's due to your recommendations.

Thank you very much for all the research you have done and are continuing to do for people with circulatory problems.

Yours truly,

A.G., USA

Dear Dr. Rath:

I am 64 years old and for four years have been suffering from heart failure, arrhythmia and shortness of breath. I had difficulty in climbing stairs and while walking I had to pause frequently. I have been following your cardiovascular health recommendations for the past two weeks.

Today I register remarkable changes: I can climb stairs without any problems. I can now walk one mile or more, even uphill. Before, I had to pause after about 200 yards. I have more energy for living.

Because of my health improvements my physician showed interest in your recommendations for cardiovascular health.

G.W., Germany

It should be noted that all these patients were severely ill heart disease patients. They were on regular medication which they were advised to continue. The reported health improvements came about when they started to take the cellular essentials. It should be noted that the amounts of cellular essentials taken were about three times the basic amounts recommended in this book.

No Heart Transplant Operation Necessary

The most dramatic success story thus far was contained in a letter I received from a patient who was so ill, that his cardiologist had put him on a waiting list for a heart transplant operation. Heart transplant operations are a capitulation of the medical profession toward a disease. "We don't know any other treatment — we have to replace the entire organ."

A frequent cause of heart disease that leads to heart transplant operations is heart failure, a weakness of the heart muscle leading to an insufficient pumping of blood. In some cases this weakness is the result of an infarction or of severe coronary heart disease. In many cases, however, the causes of this disease are unknown. The textbooks of cardiology and medicine admit: "We don't know."

The dramatic recovery of the patient whose history you will read below strongly suggests that many forms of heart failure are caused or worsened by a deficiency in cellular essentials in millions of heart cells responsible for proper blood pumping. If that is so, thousands of patients on a waiting list for heart transplant operations can immediately benefit from following this cellular essential program.

Currently 200,000 patients are on a waiting list for a heart transplant operation. For only 5,000 of them (2.5%), a suitable donor heart will be found in time. The other 195,000 will die before an operation. This simple statistic and the life-saving alternative shown below should encourage everyone who reads this book to talk about this program to neighbors, friends and colleagues — to those who have developed heart disease, but also to all those who want to prevent heart disease from developing and who would like to enjoy a long and healthy life.

G.P is an entrepreneur in his fifties. Three years ago his life was changed by a sudden occurrence of cardiac failure, a weakness of the heart muscle leading to a decreased pumping function and to an enlargement of the heart chambers. The patient could no longer fully meet his professional requirements and had to give up all his sports activities. On some days he felt so weak that he couldn't climb stairs and he had to hold his drinking glass with both hands. Because of the continued weak pumping function of the heart and the unfavorable prognosis of this disease, his cardiologist recommended a heart transplant operation: "I recommend you get a new heart."

At this point the patient started to follow my cardiovascular health recommendations. His physical strength improved gradually. Soon he could again fulfill his professional obligations on a regular basis and was able to enjoy daily bicycle rides. Two months after starting to follow my recommendations his cardiologist noted a decrease in size of the previously enlarged heart in the echocardiography examination, another sign of a recovering heart muscle. One month later the patient was able to take a business trip abroad, and he could attend to his business affairs without any physical limitations.

Encouraging Results from a Clinical Pilot Study With My Cellular Essentials Program

We wanted to know whether my cellular essentials program can objectively improve the heart performance of patients with an insufficient pumping function of their hearts (heart failure). Toward this end a clinical pilot study was carried out. If the results of this pilot study were positive, we would then conduct a large-scale study with many more patients.

Six male patients, ages 40 to 66, participated. All of them had been diagnosed with heart failure, a disease caused by a decreased pumping function of the heart, and were suffering from shortness of breath or edema. In addition to their regular medication, these patients followed a cellular essentials program for a period of two months. The amounts taken were about three times the amounts recommended as a basic program in this book.

The degree of heart failure was measured by echocardiography, the international standard procedure to assess this disease. Echocardiographic measurements of heart performance were conducted before the study, after one month and after two months of following the cellular essentials program. *The average relative increase of the heart performance in two months on a cellular essentials program was almost twenty percent (19.4%).*

In addition, the physical activity of the patient was tested in the form of exercise tests. The walking distance of the patients was measured until the onset of symptoms occurred. *The walking distance of the patients (physical performance) showed an average relative increase of more than twenty percent (21.1%) within two months of supplementation.*

The results of this pilot study allow the following conclusions:

*   A lack of cellular essentials is a cause or a contributing factor to an impaired performance of the heart (heart failure).

*   In heart failure patients, dietary supplementation with essential nutrients contained in the cellular essentials program can significantly improve heart performance.

*   In healthy people, a daily dietary supplementation with a cellular essentials program may help prevent an impairment of the heart performance and of heart failure.

*   The results of this clinical pilot study are encouraging and should be confirmed in a large-scale study. Even more so, since the heart performance improved in this pilot study with cellular essentials more than in any clinical study with prescription drugs.

Cellular Essentials Can Help Improve Heart Performance

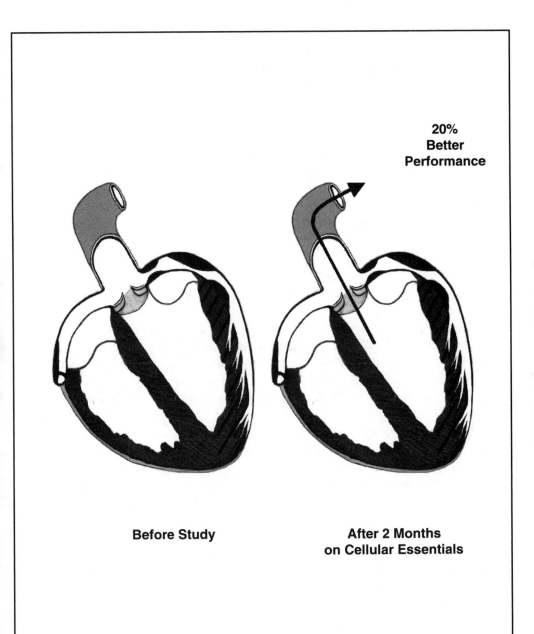

**20%
Better
Performance**

Before Study

**After 2 Months
on Cellular Essentials**

Questions and Answers

Here are some of the most frequent questions in connection with this medical breakthrough:

Q: Who needs cellular essentials?

Everyone, young and old people, men and women alike. The cellular essential program was developed as a natural preventive program to optimize cardiovascular health.

Q: Do cellular essentials replace a low-fat diet or a healthy lifestyle?

A healthy diet, moderate exercise and stress reduction are the basis of any cardiovascular health program. Cellular essentials, however, takes natural cardiovascular health a quantum leap forward. Clinical evidence shows that patients with high blood pressure, angina pectoris, irregular heartbeat, heart failure, diabetes and many other conditions can benefit from cellular essentials beyond anything achieved with lifestyle changes. Moreover, millions of people can now help to prevent these conditions with cellular essentials naturally.

Q: What is the optimum amount of cellular essentials I should take?

The recommendations in this book are a basic daily program, the minimum amounts of essential nutrients I recommend for a healthy person. People with existing cardiovascular conditions, with a family history of heart disease or with other cardiovascular risk factors may double the amounts recommended here. Alternatively, they may combine this basic formula with complementary nutritional supplement regimens according to their specific needs.

Q: When can I experience an improvement in my health condition?

There is a broad range of individual variation in response to the cellular essential program. Our documentation shows that patients with irregular heartbeat, shortness of breath and other heart disease symptoms may improve their health conditions relatively fast; although, in severe cases, it may take several months until a significant improvement is observed. Angina pectoris, the chest pain typical for coronary heart disease, my also disappear in a relatively short time because of an improved blood circulation through the coronary arteries. Three main factors contribute to this improved coronary blood flow: 1. An improved pumping function of the heart. 2. The relaxation of the coronary artery walls. 3. The reversal of atherosclerotic deposits. The first two factors can explain why in some cases angina pectoris pain disappears within a few weeks. The reversal of coronary deposits is a long-term process and takes many months or years.

Q: How safe are cellular essentials?

Very safe. All essential nutrients recommended in this book were chosen on the basis of their scientific merit - not because they were fashionable or made the news. The dosages of each ingredient is at the low end of a broad safety range. The key to any health benefit is to chose the right combination of essential nutrients in the right amounts.

Q: Should I take cellular essentials with meals or separate?

Take them with meals. By doing so you can improve the resorption particularly of the fat-soluble vitamins in the digestive tract. Also, you should take your vitamins at least twice a day, morning and evening, in order to keep the body levels of these essential nutrients at an optimum range.

Q: Should I stop taking prescription medication when following the cellular essential program?

No. Please continue your prescription medication as recommended by your doctor. Do not stop any prescription medication on your own. My recommendations for heart disease patients are as follows:

1. Start adding the cellular essentials recommended in this book to your prescription medication as soon as possible.
2. Inform your doctor about it.
3. Observe how your health improves. Take notes about your health improvements, e.g. how often you have angina pectoris or episodes of irregular heartbeat, how many stairs you can climb or how many miles you can walk without shortness of breath. During your next visit with your doctor share this information with him or her. If you can, have your blood pressure and your blood profile evaluated.
4. On the basis of these improvements your doctor may now be able to reduce your prescription medication or stop prescribing you any medication at all.
5. Please, do not stop your prescription medication on your own!

Q: Can my cholesterol level rise when taking cellular essentials?

Generally, your cholesterol levels will drop while you are on the cellular essential program. In other cases it will stay the same for some time and then gradually drop towards a normal range. In some cases, however, your cholesterol levels may even rise for a period of time until they eventually drop after several months. This effect was first reported 25 years ago by Professor Constance Spittle in the December 11, 1971, issue of The Lancet. The explanation is logical. In the blood vessel wall cellular essentials promote repair processes and thereby enhance stability. The fatty deposits in the arteries are not needed any longer and are gradually reversed. Once the blood vessel repair starts, cholesterol and other fat molecules can gradually be released from the deposits in the vessel wall into the blood stream. This is why cholesterol blood levels can rise in some patients before they eventually drop.

Q: Is there any danger when atherosclerotic deposits reverse?

No. The cellular essential program induces a gradual release of cholesterol and other fat molecules from their vessel wall deposits into the blood stream. The molecules released are much too small to cause any harm anywhere else in the circulatory system. The fat molecules released from the vessel wall are than gradually burnt in the liver. This is a biological process and not comparable to mechanical or surgical procedures such as angioplasty where the mechanical manipulation can lead to complications such as clogging.

Q: Is there a comparable cardiovascular health program?

The cellular essential program combined with a healthy lifestyle is America's most successful cardiovascular health program. Many thousands Americans already follow this program on a day to day basis because they experience the benefits for themselves. This program is easy to follow and simply the smartest way to help optimize cardiovascular health naturally for everyone.

Interview With Dr. Rath

The following interview with Dr. Rath was conducted by Jeffrey C. Kamradt.

Q: Dr. Rath, can you summarize the medical breakthrough you have led?

Dr. Rath: Yes. In simple words, my work helped to solve some of the greatest puzzles in cardiology today. Because of this work we are now able to understand the most striking medical problems which nobody could explain before. First, why animals don't get heart attacks — but humans do. Second, why people get infarctions in the arteries of their heart but rarely have infarctions in the arteries of their nose, fingers or any other parts of their body. Third, why all inherited disorders and all risk factors leading to cardiovascular diseases are closely associated with vitamin deficiencies and, as a consequence, why heart disease can be largely controlled by optimum intake of nutritional supplements. My research will help to realize an old dream of mankind: the reversal of cardiovascular disease in a natural way — without angioplasty and bypass surgery. Finally, I developed a scientifically based nutritional program that contains all the vitamins and other cellular essentials known to optimize cardiovascular health. Thousands of people are already benefiting from my nutritional programs.

Q: The problems you solved seemed so obvious and the answers to them so logical. Is there any reason why these answers were not found long ago?

Dr. Rath: Yes, in fact there are two main reasons. An economic one and the power of scientific dogmas. Vitamins are generally not patentable and there was little economic incentive for pharmaceutical companies and other health care suppliers to invest into research and clinical studies with penny substances. As a result, the real power of vitamins to maintain and restore human health was swept under the carpet of negligence and oblivion. In contrast, cholesterol-lowering drugs, for example, are a multi-billion-dollar market in the United States and, as a direct result, everyone has heard about cholesterol.

The second reason has to do with scientific dogmas. Currently, cardiovascular disease in the medical and scientific community is considered a disease largely predetermined by your family history and by your molecules of inheritance; to some extent also by lifestyle factors. Our new understanding turns upside down. We know today that heart disease is not a magic verdict but an overshooting healing process of the vessel walls. We understand that the underlying problem is the instability of the blood vessel wall caused by vitamin deficiency. Logically, we have to conclude that heart disease, by its very nature, is a preventable and a reversible disease. The key is to maintain and restore the stability of the blood vessel wall by an optimum intake of vitamins and other essential nutrients.

It will be difficult for many doctors and scientists to accept this new understanding because they have practiced medicine over many years based on existing dogmas and belief systems. The striking logic and rapidly emerging scientific evidence, however, will help doctors, scientists and millions of people around the world to accept this new understanding. As a result, millions of people will start to supplement their diet with the right essential nutrients in optimum amounts.

Q: Dr. Rath, what led you to this medical breakthrough?

Dr. Rath: Several factors may have played a role. Curiosity, a critical mind, and the ability to identify some of the main unsolved questions in medicine. A little luck was also involved, to be at the right place at the right time. Most important, however, was determination. Once I had identified the goal, I was determined to go for it, against all odds. Let me tell you some of the scientific milestones of my life:

After graduating from Hamburg Medical School in Germany I went into research to study a new risk factor, lipoprotein(a), in human blood vessels. Together with my colleagues at Hamburg University we conducted the most comprehensive studies to date on this new risk factor and its important role for the development of cardiovascular disease. By 1989 there were four people in the world who knew that it is not primarily cholesterol that causes the death of millions of people, but the adhesive lipoprotein(a) fat molecule.

In 1987 I discovered the connection between lipoprotein(a) and vitamin C. Living beings which synthesize their own vitamin C don't have and apparently don't need lipoprotein(a) and vice versa. Some of my colleagues thought it was a crazy idea. I pursued this idea and it turned out to be the first important step for this medical breakthrough.

Subsequently, I joined Linus Pauling who had seen the potential of this discovery and had encouraged me to go on. My colleagues told me that I would ruin my career by joining the maverick Linus Pauling. I went on and completed the work. The basic discovery of this scientific drive is strikingly simple: heart attacks and strokes are a form of early scurvy. Albert Einstein was right when he said: "Most of the fundamental ideas of science are essentially simple, and may be expressed in a language comprehensible to everyone." The solution to the heart disease puzzle is no exception.

Q: One would think that scientific breakthroughs such as the eradication of heart disease would be made by senior scientists or Nobel Laureates. You are only 39 years old ?

Dr. Rath: Well, your question touches on an amazing fact. Many fundamental breakthroughs in science and in history were made by young people. Apparently it is important that your mind is still fresh and not burdened with the current dogmas and belief systems. Let me give you a few examples:

Christopher Columbus was 41 when he sailed into the unknown ocean to discover America. Isaac Newton was 24 when he formulated the laws of gravitation, explaining for the first time that the tides in the oceans on earth were caused by the attraction forces of the moon. Einstein was 25 when he formulated his famous equation "$E=mc^2$," the formula that led to the nuclear bomb. James Watson was 23 when he solved the structure of the genetic code together with his colleague Francis Crick. Of course, I am not comparing myself with these great men of science. The fact remains, however, that many fundamental breakthroughs in science and history were made by young, single-minded and determined people who were ready to leave everything behind. I think this is an encouraging message for young people in many areas of life.

Q: Dr. Rath, can you tell us about your medical background and about your current work?

Dr. Rath: Certainly. I am a Medical Doctor and a member of the Chamber of Physicians in Germany. After graduating from the University of Hamburg, Germany, I held research and clinical positions at the University of Hamburg and the German Heart Center in Berlin. In 1990 I left my clinical career, because my research had become so important that I had to make a decision. As a doctor treating patients I could help 10 or 20 people per day. Finding the solution to the puzzle of heart disease would save the lives of millions of people.

The choice was clear and I came to the United States to continue the research on heart disease — not to practice medicine. In 1990 I became the first Director of Cardiovascular Research at the Linus Pauling Institute in Palo Alto, California. After leaving this Institute in 1992 I founded Health Now, a medical research and development firm specialized in the development of scientifically based nutritional products. This year we received the world's first patents to reverse heart disease without surgery. I am a member of the American Heart Association's Council on Arteriosclerosis and of the American Association for the Advancement of Science.

Q: That is exciting. Can you also share with us some of your personal background?

Dr. Rath. My background is very modest. My father was a farmer in southern Germany. He wanted me to become a farmer too, but I had other plans. I remember my father as a very humanitarian person. For example, he was head of the local YMCA until his late forties. These humanitarian values influence my own life until today and they will be a driving force for the things I set out to do in the future.

Professionally, I wanted to become a doctor practicing medicine in a third-world country and I actually planned a dissertation in tropical medicine. It soon became clear to me that there are major unsolved health problems in my own country and in the industrialized world in general. 12 million people are dying every year from heart attacks, strokes and other forms of cardiovascular diseases. This was the greatest challenge in medicine and I decided to work in this area.

I am in the privileged position to have contributed to the solution of this major health problem of our time. Looking back, my life is also an example in another way. You don't have to be born privileged — the only limits you have are the size of your ideas and the degree of your dedication.

Thank you, Dr. Rath.

Dr. Rath with the late Dr. Linus Pauling and his secretary, Mrs. Munro.

The Legacy of Dr. Linus Pauling

CALL FOR AN INTERNATIONAL EFFORT TO ABOLISH HEART DISEASE

Heart disease, stroke, and other forms of cardiovascular disease now kill millions of people every year and cause millions more to be disabled. There now exists the opportunity to reduce greatly this toll of death and disability by the optimum dietary supplementation with vitamins and other essential nutrients.

During recent years we and our associates have made two remarkable discoveries. One is that the primary cause of heart disease is the insufficient intake of ascorbate (vitamin C), an insufficiency from which nearly every person on earth suffers. Ascorbate deficiency leads to weakness of the walls of the arteries and to the initiation of the atherosclerotic process, particularly in stressed regions. We conclude that cholesterol and other blood risk factors increase the risk for heart disease only if the wall of the artery is weakened by ascorbate deficiency.

The other discovery is that the main cholesterol transporting particle forming atherosclerotic plaques is not LDL (low density lipoprotein) but a related lipoprotein, lipoprotein(a). Moreover, certain essential nutrients, especially the amino acid L-lysine, can block the deposition of this lipoprotein and may even reduce existing plaques. We have concluded that the optimum supplementation of ascorbate and some other nutrients could largely prevent heart disease and stroke and be effective in treating existing disease. Published clinical and epidemiological data support this conclusion.

The goal is now in sight: the abolition of heart disease as the cause of disability and mortality for the present generation and future generations of human beings.

WITH MILLIONS OF LIVES EACH YEAR AT STAKE NO TIME SHOULD BE LOST!

We call upon our colleagues in science and medicine to join in a vigorous international effort, on the levels of both basic research and clinical studies, to investigate the value of vitamin C and other nutrients in controlling heart disease.

We call upon the national and international health authorities and other health institutions to support this effort with political and financial measures.

We call upon every human being to encourage local medical institutions and physicians to take an active part in this process.

THE GOAL OF ELIMINATING HEART DISEASE AS THE MAJOR CAUSE OF DEATH AND DISABILITY IS NOW IN SIGHT!

Matthias Rath and Linus Pauling

- **This is the last public appeal by two-time Nobel Laureate Linus Pauling.**
- **It is a dramatic appeal to the scientific community and to the world.**
- **With this appeal Dr. Pauling supported the breakthrough toward the eradication of heart disease reported in this book.**
- **With this historic document the Nobel Laureate passed on the torch to the next generation.**
- **This historic document is handwritten by Dr. Pauling himself and signed by him in the name of two individual scientists, Dr. Pauling and Dr. Rath.**

A Call for an International Effort to Abolish Heart Disease

Heart disease, stroke, and other forms of cardiovascular disease now kill millions of people every year and cause millions more to be disabled. There now exists the opportunity to reduce greatly this toll of death and disability by the optimum dietary supplementation with vitamins and other essential nutrients.

We call upon the national and international health authorities and other health institutions to support this effort with political and financial measures.

We call upon every human being to encourage physicians and medical institutions to take an active part in this process.

THE GOAL OF ELIMINATING HEART DISEASE AS THE MAJOR CAUSE OF DEATH AND DISABILITY IS NOW IN SIGHT!

Matthias Rath and Linus Pauling

Continuing the Life Work of Dr. Linus Pauling

AGREEMENT

This is an Agreement between Dr. Matthias Rath and the Linus Pauling Institute of Science and Medicine (LPI), located at 440 Page Mill Road, Palo Alto, California 94306.

Dr. Rath joined LPI in Palo Alto in February 1990.

Dr. Rath brought to LPI the research project on cardiovascular diseases, vitamin C and Lipoprotein(a) and further pursued this program at LPI.

It is mutually understood that this research project was originated by and belongs to Dr. Rath. LPI has greatly benefited from this project with respect to an improvement in its reputation, as well as its financial support.

It is agreed that the Linus Pauling Institute waives to Dr. Rath all interests in this project and the work of Dr. Rath during his employment at LPI. This waiver includes all research data, patent rights, publications, intellectual property and material and non-material issues of any kind.

It is understood that Dr. Rath will further develop this project and thereby continue the life work of Dr. Linus Pauling.

This Agreement supersedes all previous agreements between the parties on this issue.

This Agreement shall be construed and take effect in accordance with the laws of the State of California.

22 July 1992
Date

Dr. Linus Pauling
President and
Chairman, Board of Trustees
Linus Pauling Institute

7/22/92
Date

Stephen D. Maddox
Managing Director
Linus Pauling Institute

7/ 22/92
Date

Dr. Matthias Rath

References and Sources

• A comprehensive list of references, including all studies referred to in this book, are given in my book *Eradicating Heart Disease* (see ad).
• Pictures and figures used in this book are from the following sources:
  • *Eradicating Heart Disease*
  • *Biochemistry,* Lubert Stryer, 3rd edition, W.H. Freeman and Co., New York
  • *Molecular Biology of the Cell,* Alberts B. et al. eds., Garland Publ., New York
  • *Tissues and Organs,* R.G. Kessel, R.H. Kardon, W.H. Freeman and Co.

The Comprehensive Background Information
- 200 Pages -

The Practical Handbook
- 70 Pages -

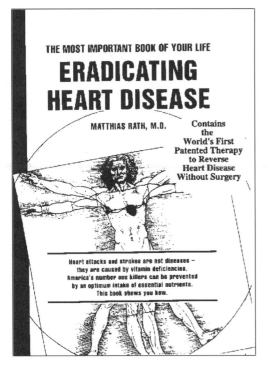

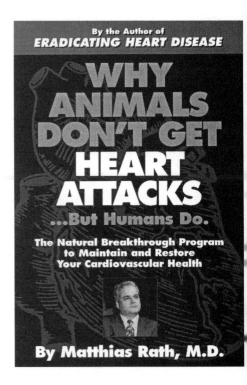

Only $14.95

Only $7.95

If you can not find these books at your local booksto you can call or write to:

Health Now
387 Ivy Street
San Francisco, CA 94102 USA
1-800-624-2442

Keep Your Cardiovascular Health Up To Date by Ordering Health Now's Cardiovascular Newsletter!

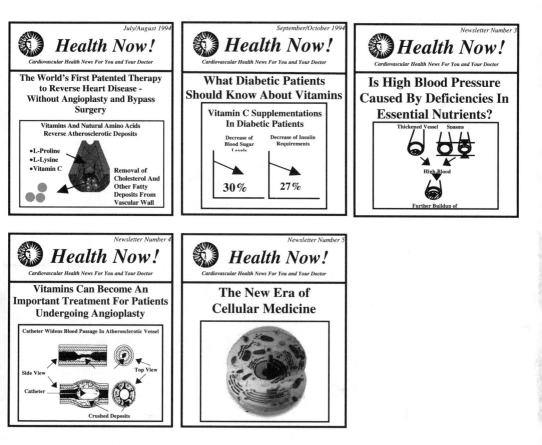

Please send me a one year subscription (six issues), bi-monthly of _Health Now's Cardiovascular Newsletter_ for $18.95

Call or Write to: